Nothing More to Lose

Carolyn Martin

A Publication of The Poetry Box®

©2021 Carolyn Martin
All rights reserved.

Editing & book design by Shawn Aveningo Sanders.
Cover design by Shawn Aveningo Sanders, using photo of Therese Kolbert Deiringer's stained glass artwork, which was gifted to Carolyn Martin & Kathy Richard.
Author's photo by Kathy Richard.
Stained glass photo by Carolyn Martin.
Images throughout this book provided by Therese Kolbert Dieringer.
These poems are based on Therese Kolbert Dieringer's autobiography, *My Life — Lived and Remembered: A journey across Hungary, Germany, and America.*

No part of this book may be reproduced in any manner whatsoever without permission from the author, except in the case of brief quotations embodied in critical essays, reviews and articles.

ISBN: 978-1-948461-78-8
Printed in the United States of America.
Wholesale distribution via Ingram.

Published by The Poetry Box®, 2021
Portland, Oregon
ThePoetryBox.com

For Therese Kolbert Dieringer who prevailed with extraordinary courage, strength, and faith.

Contents

Introduction	7
Danger	11
Who knew an angel wore a Nazi uniform?	14
Inferno	15
Cruelty and Kindness #1	16
The Searchers	18
The War Is Ending	19
Cruelty and Kindness #2	20
The School's First Refugee	21
Saved by An American Dump Yard	22
Two More Mouths to Feed	23
In the Munich Holding Camp	25
Who knew an angel had an old man's voice?	26
My Mother's Satchel Whispers	28
Liberty	29
Finding Home in Los Angeles	30
Rough Times at Bishop Conaty High	32
Mister Dance	34
This Is Hard to Admit	35
Cruelty and Kindness #3	36
How I Met Corky Dieringer	38
Corky Saves Me and My Calf	40
From the Nazis and Stalinists to the Communists	42
To Vienna with Strangers	45
Why	46
Nothing More to Lose	48

Notes	51
Praise for *Nothing More to Lose*	57
About the Author	59
About The Poetry Box®	60

Introduction

It all begins with a story on September 1, 2007. Therese is in her Vancouver, Washington kitchen filling plates with her exquisite Hungarian food. She's feeding more than 200 people—friends and family from Germany, California, and Oregon—who have flooded her backyard to celebrate her husband Corky on his 80th birthday.

She only has time for one story, maybe two, but that's enough to light the imagination of Kathy Richard, a family friend. "I want to hear more," Kathy says, and Therese invites her to lunch once festivities are over and visitors have gone home.

Kathy tells Therese she has a writer friend who could help organize her narratives. I meet Therese and am immediately engaged by the beauty, talent, and strength of a woman who has endured so much. It only takes one lunch of the best Hungarian food on the West Coast to birth the idea of a book. A book that would become Therese's legacy to her children and grandchildren.

We create a process that works for all of us. Kathy and I settle down in Therese's beautifully appointed living room. We clip a mic on her dress, check the volume on the recorder, make sure the tape is queued up, and say, "Therese, talk."

And talk she does. Hours and hours of stories pour out of her voracious memory. We sit there in horror and in awe as we learn what she and her family endured from the time they left Hungary in 1944 to their seven years of starvation and sickness in Germany to the time they arrive in Los Angeles in 1952. Immigrants, they don't know the language or landscape. This: a family of five who make a new life in a strange land with their resilience, persistence, strength, and faith.

Five recording sessions, that's what it takes. I transcribe each one, organize the stories, suggest revisions, and send manuscripts to Therese for her input. After months of backs-and-forths, we self-publish Therese's autobiography: *My Life – Lived and Remembered: A journey across Hungary, Germany, and America* in 2008.

Which brings me to this poetry collection. For several years I toyed with the idea of writing poems inspired by Therese's life, but I wasn't keen on delving into World War II history. I love doing research for my poems, but this seemed too daunting a task. And, then, it hit me hard: If I am writing poems based on Therese's experiences, this is what I need: her voice, her travels, her people, her reactions, her thoughts, her language. Of course, I'd throw some imagination in, but all the material for a chapbook was right there in the pages of the autobiography I helped create. So, as soon as I finished the first poem called "Danger," I sent it to Therese to get her reaction. I also wanted her blessing on a book that would undoubtedly bring back painful memories. With tears in her eyes and voice, she said *yes* to the poem and to a collection.

So here we are. With thanks to Kathy Richard for listening to every draft of every poem and to Shawn Aveningo Sanders, Robert Sanders, and The Poetry Box®, I am privileged to offer you *Nothing More to Lose*. I hope you can feel what I felt when I first heard Therese's stories thirteen years ago. They still make me cry and make me believe that, even in the worst of times, people can be kind. They also remind me of the power of extraordinary faith flowing through ordinary people like Therese's family.

I hope you love this book, Therese, as much as I loved writing it.

"I want you to know this is how I remembered it; what I remembered happened. It's not necessarily what happened, but close enough. I was seven at the time when all hell broke loose."

~Therese Kolbert Dieringer,
*My Life — Lived and Remembered:
A journey across Hungary, Germany, and America*

Danger

I was raised to be afraid.
~Therese Kolbert Dieringer

1. Pecs, Hungary, 1939–1944

First came the drunken Serbians—
ugly, border-crossing hooligans—
pillaging the little life we owned.

Next, peddlers of cloth, wooden spoons,
pots, and pans in child-stealing caravans
doing what they're bound to do.

Then air raids ripping through a town
not worth a bomb, scurrying us
down cellar steps where mother slept

with her satchel full of documents,
father with his file-cutting tools.
I filled the darkness in between.

Last: Nazi soldiers marching through
our streets with voices so beautiful
I fell in love with songs I didn't understand.

How could a child of seven know death
comes disguised as melodies playing
over cracked cobblestones?

*

I want one! I cried in my mother's arms:
the yellow star I tried to rip off a playmate's coat.
This: the morning playing outside ceased.

*

Trucks rolled through every night,
muting screams of yellow stars.

Why do stars disappear? I asked.
My Catholic mother could not say.

Three officers—blond, blue-eyed,
armed— quartered in our home.

No children of his own, the eldest
sat me on his lap and sang.

Hitler lost, he knew. Stalin on the way.
To Dresden: his plan for our escape.

Warm clothes, poultry, flour sacks, butchered
pigs in a railroad car marked "Classified."

Money gets you nowhere,
blue eyes said. *Food is currency.*

A 10-hour trip took three weeks.
My father stayed behind.

2. From Pecs to Dresden, 1944

The route was straight, we thought.

Except for bombings, re-routes, stalls,
screaming, crying, whining day and night.
Sleep on straw, pee through holes,
break the darkness once a day:
Red Cross soup slides through the sliding door.

Then the Vienna stop. Soldiers yank us out.
Grenades shatter cars and gypsy body parts
stain the air. We are next to die.
"Classified" does not translate.

But sirens translate into Allied bombs
that hit and hit and hit the blue Danube.
Nazis run. We run. Three hours bunkered
in the dark with anguish and despair.

For years beyond in America,
sneering kids would taunt, *She bleached her hair.*
They didn't see humans blown apart
or trains rubbled to the ground.
They didn't hear my mother scream
when she freed me from her arms
and saw her child's hair turned white.

Who knew an angel wore a Nazi uniform?

~János Kolbert

From Pecs to Dresden, November 1944

I stayed behind and hid out with our blue-eyed friend.
Stalin and Death searched for him as certain
as they searched for me. He planned our escape
in a freight car filled with machinery and straw,
crushed me in between wheels and gears and grease,
covered me with smells of sunshine and manure.

You're hiding someone, German soldiers hopped
on the train, accusing him of treachery.
No one, I swear, his protest. *I swear no one's here.*
They kicked their way around the car.
Worn-down boots barely missed my life.
I prayed without a breath.
Rants ceased. Silence. Then one shot.

I never heard my Nazi's voice again.

Inferno
Dresden, February 13, 1945

My father goes to work every day.
Blindfolded, bussed for miles away from our lives
on the outskirts of culture and history.

Lowered underground into artificial light.
Eight-hour shifts building airplanes
for Hitler's lost campaign.

Who knows why he refused to go that day—
rumors, angels, rumblings in his gut?—
and risked being shot for staying home.
I would rather die with my family,
he stands his ground. His frantic wife cries.
We go to bed terrified of German guns
bursting through our doors.

No comfort of sleep before sirens scream
and Allied planes send hell from the skies.
Fire invades everything, turning blind night
into blinding day. We scramble down
our sloping yard into the creek below.
Wading in the wet saves our lives.

At dawn, my father carries me,
my mother clutches her case.
Along with caravans of stunned souls,
we pass the body-bloated Elbe
and stumble onto railroad tracks.

Days and days and days before we find
a train heading west, bound for seven
starving years in the madness of Germany.

Cruelty and Kindness, #1
Dillingen, Germany 1945

The war rages on and my parents toil for food:
500 calories a day. *Too much to die with,*
my father sighs. *Too little to live on.*

On a rich estate, my mother works
the kitchen, my father the farm.
Five in the morning until after dark.

And I'm a lonely kid. No one talks to me.
But I find entertainment through a hole
in a fence. It's heaven to watch

a girl my age playing by herself
with a doll and some toys. For hours
on end I never make a sound. Then ...

her mother finds me, calls me the lowest
of the low, beats me and beats me again.
Why must we feed nothings like you?

*

I stop eating, stay in bed, start
to cough and cough and cough.
If we don't leave, she'll die, my father says.

He picks me up, my mother grabs her case.
We walk pass German guards who know
how TB sounds. They don't shoot. They let us go.

*

Another part of town, another job
sheltered in an empty blacksmith shop
filled with rats and mice.

My mother finds a sunshine patch
near another fence. Another stranger
on the other side hears me cough.

The woman says, *I don't have much.
Two goats and some milk.* My mother swears,
Better than drugs. Milk heals my lungs.

*

The goat lady says, *Your child needs school.*
The only one: a convent school where sweet nuns
give this coughing child gentle strokes
and the patience she hungers for.

But we don't stay here for long.
What you need to know: in the clutches
of terror, sickness, and hunger pangs,
I blur my days into weeks, weeks into months.

The Searchers

Every week we went looking for relatives in refugee camps.
~János Kolbert

For Toni, my friend Frank Mûller's 12-year-old. We find him in a Leipzig orphanage covered with sores oozing worms. His mother faints at first sight. My wife nurtures and heals and returns him to his mother's arms.

For Ferenz, my mirror twin, sent to the Russian front. In Dachau we hear he's on a train headed back to Hungary. He thinks we are there. We're running down the tracks shouting his name, shouting, *Your family is here!* With people so crammed in, he can't get out. We miss him by a moment and a platform's length. Back home, the Russians capture him. Three more years before he escapes to find us again.

For Anna, Frank's daughter, shipped to the Caucuses to work in Russian salt mines. She escapes and finds us before we find her. Let me tell you how: You know where trains couple each to each? She hides underneath, holding on with legs and arms—frost bite everywhere. It takes a year for her to get back to Hungary, but we're not there. Soldiers in our house. All of us gone. She finds my mother who knows our address. What's left of Anna walks into our German yard. She's seventeen.

Millions of refugees never find their homes. We are lucky to find three.

The War Is Ending
Burghagel, Germany 1945

And it is still horrible.
We'd be walking anywhere
when suddenly Allied planes would fly so low
we could almost touch their wings,
almost feel their engines' heat.

They couldn't see Hungarian eyes—
or Yugoslavs' or Ukrainians'.
They'd shoot anyone in sight.
We'd dive into ditches, hide in piles
of manure. Anywhere to stay alive.

Then the first wave of Americans.
For hours black soldiers march through town.
I never saw a black person before,
never knew there was such a thing.
Americans are black! my child's first thought.

I remember their big tanks and big smiles,
their snipers guarding their men going house
to house, routing German soldiers out.
The rest of us? Left unharmed, untraumatized.

I have to tell you this: when war is war,
horror comes in many forms.
I saw the Germans in Hungary,
I saw the Russians everywhere.
But the Amies'* army?
Commendable above the rest.

* A nickname for Americans

Cruelty and Kindness, #2
Ottobrunn 1946

Another town, another job.
This one with a rich Nazi buying
his way out of punishment.
A bribe here, a greased palm there.
His kind was everywhere.

We lived in filthy barracks where bed bugs
bit my dad, poisoned his blood,
sent him into feverish delirium.

The Nazi and his men came to pull him out.
No lazy bums in this establishment!
My mother begged for help. What she got?
My father beaten up and thrown out the gates.
The sidewalk was piled with snow.

A scrawny kid, skin and bones, I tried
to keep him warm. I held him in my arms
and sang and struggled to pray.
My mother walked two miles to find a train.

*

A stranger heard my mother's sobs.
Grabbed a taxi, came to pick us up,
took us to his home a town away.

And there was warmth and furniture
and powdered scrambled eggs—
Heaven! We hadn't eaten for days!
And there was a doctor for my dad
and new work on the American airbase.
We stayed from winter into spring.

The School's First Refugee
Ottobrunn 1947

*If you have to have a horrible life, have it as a kid.
The young deal with it better.*
~Therese Kolbert Dieringer

No books or pencils for 79 kids.
We sat on floors and windowsills
and learned from the blackboard
and the rigid teacher's voice.
She scared the daylights out of us.

Four times five minus six divided by seven,
she'd demand and we'd answer back—or else.

And when class was out, the beatings began.
Kids came at me like wasps. Chunks of hair
ripped out, eyes swollen shut.
The teacher stood on the stairs and watched.
Too many beatings for me to tally up.

Saved by An American Dump Yard
1947–1950

For seven years I went to bed hungry and got up hungry.
~Therese Kolbert Dieringer

We'd run to the yard every day and wait
for airbase trucks to dump their trash.
When you're starving and ration cards
don't provide, you'll eat anything—
from pieces of donut cake to piles
of chicken heads and chicken feet:
treasures in the Amies' throw-aways.

Later, we learn to scout the streets
for cigarettes. Soldiers love to smoke
and throw their butts away.
My father makes packets of tobacco flakes:
the best for black-market trades.
They buy us shoes and bread.

Later, I lug home wooden crates,
cut them into kindling wood.
House to house I go where soldiers lived
with wives. One bundle earns a bar of soap
or chocolate or a loaf of bread—
anything they didn't want.
Then I win the lottery: a blanket, gold and green.
It turns into a coat: the first warmth in years.
Made for Amies, cherished by a refugee.

Two More Mouths to Feed
Winter 1947

My mother's swollen belly doesn't mean a thing—
mine is swollen, too.
But when the ambulance arrives
and they put her in,
She's going to die! I cry frantically.

Put on your coat, my father snaps me back.
We plow through piles of snow to catch
the Munich train. I almost freeze to death.

Ten minutes in the hospital, not more,
when this fluttering little nun runs at us.
Herr Kolbert! Herr Kolbert! You have a daughter!

Of course he has a daughter, I think.
I'm right here! What I want to know:
Is my mother dead? No one talks to me.

Moments later, the flutter is back.
Herr Kolbert! Herr Kolbert! You have a son!
She raises two fingers above her smiling face.
My father passes out.

She's killed him, I thought, and I am on her
like a fly on shit. I scratch and bite and tear.
It takes three of them to pull me off.

Smelling salts bring him back
and he takes my hand, leads me
to my mother and the twins: tiny, blue,
uglier than anything I'd ever seen.
Three pounds; three-and-a-half.
My mother's body keeps them warm.

To tell you the truth,
I fell into the deepest shock
that three months pass by
and I don't remember much.
What I am told: at one month,
pneumonia sets in. Nine days and nights
taking turns, we walk the twins around
a cabin so cold ice crystals glisten
on the walls, water freezes in the cream can
near the blazing stove.
Their only warmth: our body heat.

They tell me those two hungry mouths
get well just before diphtheria finds me again.

I do remember this: three more years of sicknesses.
Whooping cough, fevers—scarlet and typhoid.
Three kids in hospitals for weeks that turn to months.

Decades later in America, I will look
into the twin's sweet eyes.
Rosie and Johnny, I will say,
I am so proud of you. How we all survived!

In the Munich Holding Camp
1952

The Germans couldn't wait to kick us out.
Too many starving mouths, too much sickness and death.
So they made a deal: they'd build holding camps
and Americans would screen the likes of us,
then ship us off to any state with jobs and roofs.

Three months in Munich: 30-40 to a room.
Evenings we'd learn American songs
and watch cowboys shoot it out on dusty streets,
ride across red landscapes we had no concept of.

Sometimes we'd hear the Philharmonic play
the classics in the Kaiserplatz,
and, if we could find a way,
we'd get a seat in the Munich opera.

What we didn't know: a Catholic priest
in Los Angeles is finding lodging
and work for 40,000 refugees.
900 at a time. We are five.

Who knew an angel had an old man's voice?

This is how it was: Americans fighting
the Korean war. Their ships drop men off
and pick up refugees on their way back home.
So we get on a soldier ship and it is good.

I can't forget my mother gathering us
in her arms, looking back at land
as the ship pulls away. *I'll never set foot,*
she vows, *on this continent again.*
She kept her word.

    *

The first night: hot dogs and sauerkraut.
I'd never seen a hot dog before,
hadn't eaten meat in years.
Now here was all this food
and showers three times a week.
I'd never seen a shower in my life.
With 900 on board, what they thought
was water-rationing is heaven to me.

    *

The third night out they had a dance.
I fluffed up best I could because I loved
to dance and boys would be there.
But at the door, they wouldn't let me in.
Fourteen. Too young. They blocked my way.

Oh, the upset and the tears and the moping
around the deck until an old man
called out, *Little girl, stop your slobbering.
Go to bed right now. Tomorrow*

you'll be glad you didn't eat or drink.
Bloody rude! I thought, but listened to his words.

What the old man knew from experience:
our glide through the English Channel was about
to turn into a raucous ride across the open seas.

Next morning such a sight!
People everywhere holding brown bags,
looking green. For the rest of the trip—
eight days turned into twelve—
nobody came to breakfast,
few showed up at dinner time.
The twins and I and Johnny, my good friend,
ate and ate and ate. We never got sick.
We could take ten showers a day
if we wanted to.

My Mother's Satchel Whispers

From beside your bed
on this seasick ship,
I listen to you moan and pray.
I wonder if you can smell
Dresden death
seeping through my seams
and hear the sounds of bombs,
screams, and labor pains
echoing through
the darkness in between
your documents.
I remember how
you clutched me tight
and rescued me
from blood-stained tracks,
rats and snow,
the taunts of brutal men.
And when János said,
We must go,
you never thought twice.
The heavier I got,
I never feared
you'd leave me behind.
We were wedded each to each,
my sweet, steady woman.
My companion, my guardian.
What can I give you
as we plow through
unsteady storms
toward The Promised Land?
The only thing I have:
the vow we made
to protect your memories
until we both wear out.

Liberty
May 1952

The sun was coming up as we pulled into the harbor, just in that red stage, hitting the Statue of Liberty. We had reached the Promised Land after this long twelve-day journey with storms and seasickness. My mother was very weak. There were so many sick people staggering around. But, because I was blessed enough not to get sick, Johnny and I and the kids and a few others were up there watching this. I have to say that even though I was a child, it was something that I'll never forget. We pulled into Ellis Island and we were met with hot chocolate and cake donuts....

We disembarked and, as we left the ship, we were handed an envelope. It had a picture of [our ship], the General Blatchford, in it. I still have this picture in my bedroom because my mother saved it....

We went through Ellis Island pretty quickly. In my recollection, it didn't take more than three hours. There were taxi cabs waiting for us and all several hundred of us were taken by cab to Grand Central Station. Mind you, this country bumpkin who had never seen anything bigger than Bremen and Munich and all the other big bombed-out cities, and here I am in the skyscraper area looking up and running outside. I was trying to count the stories. By the time I got to thirty-six, I was so dizzy!

Finding Home in Los Angeles
May–August 1952

Another train west. Five days
and three hundred refugees
land on St. Stephen's steps
and I could smell paprika before I saw
the Hungarian mamas' welcoming:
a soup/chicken/noodles/salad spread.

And that's the way it was:
the already settled-in helping the latest transports.
It was word-of-mouth: who to talk to, where to go.
When you don't know language or landscape,
the going is impossible.

Ten days in a Jewish hotel while my dad looks
for work and I walk the streets learning fast
what "For Rent. No Children" means.

Then "For Rent: Furnished":
a kitchen, bedroom, bath, roll-out bed,
shelves of glasses, plates, cooking ware.
We move in with three suitcases full
of clothes and the satchel that crossed
every mile of seven years. Life is good.

*

One night my bed starts to roll
and people are screaming and sirens howling
and streets filling with pajamas and nightgowns
and transformers exploding everywhere
and I am back in Dresden again.
Bombs, I think. This night: my first earthquake.

*

Our priest gets me a summer job: babysitting
two kids for a soldier and his teacher wife.
I need to learn English fast. Only two weeks in LA,
I can't communicate, but the mother shows me
what to do and we get on well.

I cook better than she can,
out-perform their washing machine,
and hang their laundry in fresh air.

The more I do, the more she trusts me with.
Like the morning she hands me a note:
a number and a name. I don't know
what it means but, suitcases in their car,
they are gone for a week. We have plenty
of food and the milkman comes every day.

And the kids! They are fascinated
by this fourteen-year-old who knows how to play.
And the summer is good. The little ones pick up
German fast, while the English I was supposed
to learn goes nowhere. School is only weeks away.

Rough Times at Bishop Conaty High
1953–1954

Why I never know, but the principal—
no sweet nun—has it in for me
and tries and tries to kick me out.
First, for tiny earrings I'd worn since birth:
rubies a jeweler fastened so they won't get lost.
Even soldiers couldn't steal them
from my ears in their holding camps.

Mind you, three thousand girls in school—
big hooped earrings everywhere—
and my little ones anger her.
Nazis never bothered me like this.

And there are the sandals I wear.
For her, my defiance of the school's uniform.
But my toenails are so ingrown,
my toes are purple plums.

One day on the walk to school,
I pass out—what are the odds?—
in front of a podiatrist shop.
A nurse calls an ambulance.
Infection, blood poisoning,
surgery after surgery.

I go back to school and the nun starts in
again: *Wear your saddle shoes or else!*
I have to admit in all honesty,
if she didn't make life so miserable,
I might not have left high school
and married so young.

Mister Dance

Every morning I walk the twins to school,
then walk to school myself.
I'd pick them up, walk them home.
My father, home from work, takes care of them
so I can walk to the Five-and-Dime
to clean and dust and mop until 10 p.m.
Then home to homework and sleep.
Start the next day again, walking everywhere.

But the weekends are for fun.
My father and I walk to gatherings—
German and Hungarian. He teaches
all my friends to dance and dances with everyone.
Papa Kolbert is "Mister Dance."

And so is Karl, a blue-eyed blond,
I meet in church. He is everything
on my must-have list: a lover of song
and dance, part of my culture and background,
my escape from years of overwork
and moving around.

I leave school to marry him.
It's 1955. I'm seventeen and naïve.
Who knew Karl is a Nazi with an angel's face?
I learn too much, I learn too late.

This is Hard to Admit
1955–1981

I married and divorced,
not once but twice,
the same womanizing man.

It would take more
than a poet—
a novelist, playwright,
and psychologist, perhaps—
to explain twenty-six years
of taunts, abuse, and misery.

All he left behind:
three cherished children
who became my life.

Cruelty and Kindness #3
Scotts Mills, Oregon 1963–1981

The Swiss-German community
arrives at our new farm in a car caravan.
Food, a keg of beer, an accordion
— a whole night of camaraderie.

A woman teaches me how to can—
900 quarts of food every year.
Two men save my cows buried in the snow.
Farmers let me work their fields
while I run my farm. To make ends meet,
I'd out berry-pick the Russians and Mexicans.
My fast hands do this for seasons to come.

*

Karl disappears all the time.
The longer we are married,
the less he does—except getting into debt
and wanting me to bail him out.

I finally stand firm and he yells and screams
at my thwarting his next scheme.
So he tries to take my life.

I'm running water in the kitchen sink,
adding soap, starting to scrub.
He comes from behind and shoves my head in.
His rage settles into quietness.

Nearby, my little girls watch horrified.
The older runs and starts to bite and kick
and threaten him. He laughs and laughs
and laughs and lets me go.

I should have put him in jail.
Another big mistake. In the eyes of a community
who doesn't know this man or what he's done,
my divorce makes me the guilty one.

I serve him papers on a Wednesday.
Sunday he's in church, sitting
in our family's pew with his latest girlfriend.

How I Met Corky Dieringer

One phone call and he is at my door,
carrying a German man I've known for years.
Mr. Wellman loved my raw potato cakes
and every Sunday after church,
he became our breakfast guest.

But I moved on and now he's facing
bone-cancer death. All he wants:
one more of my home-cooked meals.
That's what Corky says.

In his grubby farm clothes and dirty boots,
he carries Mr. Wellman in.
A six-foot-two strapping man, now
a shriveled hunchback, skin-and-bones.

We eat and talk and eat and talk
and, as they are about to leave,
Corky steps on my toe. I let out a shriek.
He picks up my foot and starts to kiss
the injury. *How insane!* I think.
What an awful man!
I never want to see him again.

*

The second phone call is just as bad.
*Are you sitting up there feeling sorry
for yourself?* It sounds like a taunt.

Believe me, there is no time for sitting
or sorrowing. I'm working my butt off
farming and taking on other jobs
to feed and school my kids.

What I learn: Corky's heart is in
the right place, but his mouth sometimes
says really stupid stuff.
What I meant, he tries to explain,
was you need to get out socially.
Relax and enjoy life again.

So it begins:
dinners and dances with friends.
A little smooch here and there.
He remains a gentleman,
racks up points, endears himself
in a million ways over the next four years.

Corky Saves Me and My Calf

68 head of cattle. Registered Black Angus.
Short legs. And 18 cows are calving
in my loafing shed.

Karl stole my tractor and blade
so I can't muck it out. Now cows are up
to their bellies in their own manure.

Home from work at 2 p.m.,
I find a mama threw her calf.
Up to its head in shit, it's being sucked in.
Think quicksand and you'll know what I mean.

I can't let this little one die, so I put on boots
and start. One step at a time. Six or seven
in agony. Then I hear his voice.

Honey, you're doing fine. Don't rush.
The mama will care for her own.
Go easy or you'll make it worse.

Corky coaches me and I finally grab the calf
covered from head to toe.
Its mama seems relieved and heads
for the pasture and fresh air.

Corky's voice urges me through my tiredness.
He's smart enough not to jump in.
Two problems won't solve this one.

I shove the calf through the rails
and Corky takes it in his arms.
Now he's filthy, too. But I'm stuck
and start to cry. There's just no strength
to turn and follow the cow out the back.

But Corky, smart farmer that he is, says,
Therese, you're so slick, I'll slide you
through these rails. I have my doubts,
but he pulls me through.

Later, he finds a machine and mucks out my barn.
Another notch in the belt tallying up his love.

From the Nazis and Stalinists to the Communists
Summer 1985

I married Corky in March and that summer we were off to Hungary, Germany, and Austria. I didn't want to go. The Iron Curtain was up. If it came down on me, I'd be lost. Understand, the US couldn't save its naturalized. If you're back in your birth country and they choose to keep you, they can. To be honest, I was terrified.

And it started right away: in Frankfurt's airport where Russian soldiers prowled with sub-machine guns. Someone canceled our flight on an American airline, put us on a Communist plane. We climbed into this World War II jet with a young punk pilot who flew us to Budapest through a lightning storm. Of course, a bolt struck us and I knew we were going to die. Corky held me tight, told me it would be all right.

It poured in Budapest and luggage was heaped on the flooded ground. We found ours and lugged it to the terminal a quarter-mile away. Corky went left into the line for native-born Americans, and I went to the right. Young soldiers started to question me, and I made my first mistake: I spoke Hungarian. Out of practice 40 years with the vocabulary of a kid, it was horrible.

They kept asking, *Why did you leave? Why did you leave?*

Exhaustion and anger finally loosened my tongue. *What are you? Morons? I was seven-years-old! Why do you think? My parents took me away.* They were not amused and told me to shut my mouth. Then they kicked me out.

I found Corky with a soldier: a huge Russian woman rifling through our bags. She's pillaging all the gifts we packed for relatives. When she fingered pairs of pantyhose, I shouted, *You are too fat for those!* She threw them in my face—the only gifts we saved.

*

But goodness finds us in a Budapest hotel. By chance we meet two Germans on holiday. They don't speak Hungarian, so I can translate. They have a car, so we can tour the sites. Four days of fun and they become friends for life.

On our last night, Corky springs a surprise. My father told him about a restaurant he remembered from youth. Leave it to Corky to arrange for a cozy room with enough Hungarian food to feed an army for a week. We start at 7:30 p.m., end at 2:30 a.m. In between, a gypsy band plays and Corky livens up the night by sending bottles of wine to the whole room. And we eat and drink and sing and laugh and create memories.

*

Then it's off to Pecs, my birthplace. We couldn't drive our rental car too fast—war-made potholes slowed us everywhere. Corky was at the wheel when a police car pulled us off the road. Four muggers with guns strode up to the driver's side. They didn't want our visas or passports. They wanted our cash. American dollars were valuable. They slammed Corky against the car, emptied his wallet, and threw it back.

My wise mother told us to hide dollars in a money belt and we were happy for her words. Forty dollars was all they got. They didn't think to pat Corky down. One guy took out a pad, wrote $40 on it. *Here's your speeding ticket*, he laughed.

As we drove away, I turned to Corky and said, *Welcome to Communism. This is what is called highway robbery.*

*

There are many more stories I could tell, but let me say this: Hungarians suffered through the Nazis. They suffered through the Stalinists. But the Communists? They were much worse

To Vienna with Strangers

You never know who you're going to help.
The Good Samaritan made his name
by caring for a stranger on a dusty road.
I believe you help no matter who shows up.
For me, that's the way it always works.

We're sitting on a depot bench
waiting for the bus, when I hear a man
and woman crying to the ticket clerk.

He's pleading in English, in Spanish,
in German, but she won't answer him.
This is Hungary. What does he expect?
She only speaks Hungarian.

I almost laugh because I know
what it's like and ask if I can help.
They kiss and hug and thank me
for seating them on our Vienna bus.

What we didn't know:
the man: a diplomat from Ecuador.
For my few words, he books us in the finest hotel,
wines and dines us every night.
Five days of Viennese luxury
for a few caring words. We don't pay a cent.
Think about it: it's almost like a parable.

Why

*My kids need to know this. The happiest years
of my life have been with Corky.*
～Therese Kolbert Dieringer

Because he knew that new love comes slowly after the terror of the old.

Because he introduced me to Coffee Nudge and I felt no pain.

Because he bought birthday corsages for wives before their husbands even thought of it.

Because he took my scared, broken self into his bathroom one day and made me look into the mirror. *Repeat after me*, he said: *Therese, you are a beautiful, wonderful person.*

Because when I said, *No!* he said, *Say it louder.* And I did.

Because he said, *Say it every morning when you wake up.* And I did.

Because my mother grew to love him like a son and told me, *No one on earth is ever going to love you more than this man.*

Because she died in his arms.

Because he admitted—months after his Budapest surprise—that he didn't wear out our credit card. Three soups, eight salads, thirteen kinds of meat, more beer and wine than I could count: $50 for four of us. He added a $50 tip.

Because, when my sister's husband was dying of cancer, he did their yardwork.

Because, when I didn't know if I was going to live or die, he loved me through breast cancer.

Because, when we realized the Scotts Mills farm was too much work, he agreed to move to a Vancouver home we could love.

Because every morning he brought me coffee in bed and repeated this litany: *Therese, my kissable love, my adorable love, my loveable love, I will love you always in all ways. You are my wife, my love, my sweetheart, my lover, my companion, my friend.*

Because he was Corky, my rock, and I miss his hugs, his kisses, and his voice.

Nothing More to Lose
Vancouver, Washington, 2020

My dear husband of thirty years dead.
My three children sheltered in their lives.
My days mostly rose beds, baking bread, memories.
My feet ache from years of too-small shoes,
my ears from bombs and screams.
My eyes try to block the fiery night we waded
in a Dresden stream; the seven years
of hunger, cold, fevers, lice in Germany.

Here in the comfort of my home—miles of time
away from that history—I place my 83-year-old life
into my father's calloused hands.
He tells me stars sing the clearest songs across the sky.
He tells me everything is very good.
He tells me there is nothing more to lose.

Notes

"Danger"

Pecs was a medieval town in southern Hungary near the Yugoslav border. It was wine and coal mining country. Therese's grandfather died in a coal-mining accident when her father János was eleven. At age twelve, János got a job in the same mine where his father died.

~Therese Kolbert Dieringer, *My Life – Lived and Remembered: A journey across Hungary, Germany, and America*, p. 1.
(All subsequent citations are from this book.)

Therese's mother kept a satchel of documents and photographs that she took with her wherever the family went. As Therese says, *She had all our papers in it: our birth certificates, every pay slip my dad ever had in his working life since he married her.... I wouldn't have pictures of our family growing up if she didn't have that suitcase.* (p. 7)

File-cutting tools: When János was seventeen, his uncle sent him to school to learn the trade. Since there were no factories to make files, they were cut by hand—from the tiniest fingernail files to seventy-pound war industry files. János became a master cutter and this skill saved him from being conscripted into the German army. The Germans needed files for their war effort. (p. 1)

The Nazi who sang to Therese almost killed her mother the first evening he and his men arrived. Eating his first Hungarian meal, he was sure Theresa Kolbert's spicy cooking was meant to poison him. Luckily, one of the other officers pushed his gun aside. The bullet hit a wall. Later he became the friend and rescuer of the family. (p. 8)

When Therese and her mother returned to the depot after the bombing, they found every freight car destroyed—except one. Their car stood intact, still holding the clothes and food that had traveled with them for weeks. (p. 11)

"Who knew an angel wore a Nazi uniform?"

János Kolbert finally arrived in Dresden with his best friend Frank Mûller right before St. Nicholas Day, December 6, 1944. The seven-year-old Therese imagined he arrived on Santa's sleigh. *And I so remember thinking,* she says, *Oh, boy! I respected that SANTA!* (p. 12)

"Inferno"

The Kolberts, like thousands of others, were classified as "civilian prisoners." Throughout their time in Germany, they worked not for wages, but for meager food and shelter.

Because he had worked in a coal mine, János, unlike many of his fellow workers, knew the feel of an elevator being lowered into the ground. The massive munitions factory beneath Dresden was the Allies' real target, not the beautiful city above. (pp. 12–13)

"The Searchers"

When the Germans invaded Hungary, Frank Mûller was conscripted into the German army. His children were put into a Hitler Youth Camp. Frank's 12-year-old son was sent to the Leipzig orphanage after being intercepted by Stalin in Poland in 1944. (p. 7)

Anna Mûller, Toni's sister, was shipped to the Caucuses and Ural Mountains by the Russians to work in the salt mines. (p. 7)

Ferenz Kolbert, János's identical twin, was also conscripted by the Germans and sent to the Russian front in 1944. He became a prisoner of the Americans when they liberated Dachau in 1945. (p. 7)

"The War Is Ending"

Burghagel was near a Hitler Youth Camp. Most likely, the Allies thought everyone on the ground was a Nazi. (p. 17)

"Cruelty and Kindness, #2"

The American airbase was located in Neubieberg, a couple of miles from Ottobrunn. The kind stranger got János a job there as a janitor. (p. 24)

"Saved by An American Dump Yard"

The dump yard was located in Ottobrunn. The trash came from the American airbase in Neubieberg.

"In the Munich Holding Camp"

Father Matthias Lany from the Diocese of Los Angeles traveled to Europe to visit refugee camps. He was so moved by the horrible conditions there, he went back to LA and convinced Bishop McIntyre to sponsor refugees. With the Bishop's blessing, he gradually brought 40,000 refugees to the United States. (p. 37)

"Liberty"

These are Therese's exact words describing this experience. (pp. 44–45)

"Finding Home in Los Angeles"

Therese's group was divided up and taken to hotels owned by a Jewish hotelier, Mr. Bauer. Most of Father Lany's friends were Jewish businessmen who became the major sponsors of the refugees. The Kolberts stayed in the hotel for ten days before they found their first apartment. (pp. 46–47)

"Rough Times at Bishop Conaty High"

János Kolbert was angry at a marriage that would end Theresa's schooling. However, she promised him she would graduate. Soon after her marriage, she entered the Manual Arts Public School and graduated at the same time as her Bishop Conaty High School class. (p. 54)

"Mister Dance"

Years into their marriage, Therese learned that Karl's father was a millionaire Nazi contractor who enrolled the young Karl in the Hitler Youth. As Therese said, *Karl learned young.* (p. 70)

"Cruelty and Kindness #3"

After negotiating the price with the elderly owner who was about to be evicted, Therese, Karl, and their son Joe moved to the Scotts Mills, Oregon, farm in 1963. It had 120 acres, a huge barn, and a ramshackle shack that was more dilapidated than anything Therese had lived in in Germany. Between the filth and the rats, it wasn't the kind of home Therese had grown accustomed to during her ten years in Los Angeles. (pp. 59–61)

To cover Karl's debts, Therese sold off 65 acres. They built a home on the last 55 acres in 1977-1978. By the time she divorced Karl in 1981, the farm had 68 head of cattle. Therese started to cook full-time at the local school. Then, in the summer, she would work in the fields and canneries. She would clean houses and sell cosmetics—all to make ends meet. When she said, *The longer were we married, the less [Karl] did,* she meant it literally. (p. 66)

Karl died in 2001. He was buried on the same day Therese learned she had breast cancer. (p. 77)

"Why"

After Therese's battle with breast cancer, she and Corky realized that they both had physical limitations that made taking care of a 55-acre farm impossible. They needed to be closer to hospitals, doctors, and their kids. In 2003, they found their Vancouver home. (p. 102)

Corky passed away on June 2, 2014, and Therese still lives in this lovely home filled with family photographs and her stained-glass artwork. The outside is surrounded by exquisite rose bushes and loving neighbors.

Praise for
Nothing More to Lose

It would seem that Carolyn Martin, the poet, and Therese Kolbert Dieringer, the persister, have become quantumly entangled—that state of essential being in which what happens to one happens to the other, what is felt by one is felt by the other, no matter any barriers of time or distance. How else to explain Therese's experiences—surviving Nazis, spousal abuse, and being found by new, liberating love—expressed with such first-hand poetic beauty by Carolyn's stirring and sterling lines? Alert Bohr and Planck! Martin and Dieringer have established the principle of poetic entanglement and extended it to us. Thomas Merton wrote, "We have all stood in front of that special image that sang to our soul." Were he alive today and asked for an example, he would hand the person this chapbook.

~Wayne-Daniel Berard,
co-founding editor of *Soul-Lit: a journal of spiritual poetry*
and author of *The Realm of Blessing*

In her introduction to *Nothing More to Lose*, Carolyn Martin says, "… even in the worst of times, people can be kind." That idea buoys these poems that share a truly horrific tale of survival beginning in WWII Hungary. Through Martin's deftly crafted images, we see into the life of Therese Kolbert Dieringer as she and her family flee Nazis, bombs, starvation, and more. The long journey that concludes in America brings Therese to a safer, but not necessarily less cruel, place. I had to take little breaks as I read these poems; that human beings are capable of causing so much pain is nearly unbearable. But Dieringer's voice comes through each of Martin's poems showing how kindness and cruelty co-exist in us all, and how true strength and resilience cannot be extinguished. Most importantly, kindness wins.

> ~ Kathleen Cassen Mickelson,
> cofounder of *Gyroscope Review*
> and blogger at *One Minnesota Writer*

In *Nothing More to Lose,* Carolyn Martin has read and written my soul. No one has been able to feel what I felt before this poet shared her inspired words with me and now with the world. I spent more than 70 years trying to forget the events that shaped my life and gave me nightmares. Now, through working with Carolyn on both my autobiography and this chapbook, I feel healed. The nightmares are gone.

I hope these poems will help readers find courage in the realization we are not here on our own. We are guided by a Higher Power. This book is a good way to end my journey.

> ~Therese Kolbert Dieringer

About the Author

From associate professor of English to management trainer to retiree, Carolyn Martin is a lover of gardening and snorkeling, feral cats and backyard birds, writing and photography. After years of producing academic papers and business books, she discovered that poetry is the way her heart and mind interact with the world —in images, rhythms, sounds, and intensities of language. So she has settled into the joyful challenge of translating experience into as few words as possible.

Martin's aesthetic is embodied in Jack Kerouac's comment in *Dharma Bums*: "One day I will find the right words, and they will be simple," and in Sting's statement, "All my life I have tried to find the truth and make it beautiful."

Her poems attempt to use simple words to embrace truths wherever she finds them, and to turn them into something approximating the beautiful.

Her poems have appeared in journals throughout North America, Australia, and the UK, and her fifth poetry collection, *The Catalog of Small Contentments*, will be released by The Poetry Box® in 2021. She is the book review editor for the Oregon Poetry Association and the poetry editor of *Kosmos Quarterly: journal for global transformation*.

<www.carolynmartinpoet.com>

About The Poetry Box®

The Poetry Box® is a boutique publishing company in Portland, Oregon, who provides a platform for both established and emerging poets to share their words with the world through beautiful printed books and chapbooks.

Feel free to visit the online bookstore (thePoetryBox.com), where you'll find more titles including:

The Way A Woman Knows by Carolyn Martin

Broadfork Farm by Tricia Knoll

Many Sparrows by donnarkevic

Like the O in Hope by Jeanne Julian

A Shape of Sky by Cathy Cain

The Very Rich Hours by Gregory Loselle

Shadow Man by Margaret Chula

Between States of Matter by Sherry Rind

November Quilt by Penelope Scambly Schott

A Long, Wide Stretch of Calm by Melanie Green

The Kingdom of Birds by Joan Colby

and more . . .

www.ingramcontent.com/pod-product-compliance
Lightning Source LLC
LaVergne TN
LVHW020437080526
838202LV00055B/5237